I Left Christianity

What Made Me Change
My Discoveries and an Alternative

A Memoir and Guide

By

Peter Newenly

Copyright © Peter Newenly 2021

All rights reserved. Other than for the purposes and subject to the conditions prescribed under the *Copyright Act*, no part of this publication may be reproduced, stored in a retrieval system, or transmitted in any form or by any means, electronic, mechanical, photocopying, recording or otherwise, without the prior permission of the publisher.

This book is a work of non-fiction

ISBN: 978-0-9873283-7-3

Cover Design by: Judith Paquin

Table of Contents

Prologue	1
Part 1 History Influences Discoveries	3
1 - Where am I Now?	5
2 - A Short Life Story	13
3 - My Process Toward Change	23
4 - Past Influences That Guided My Change	29
• The Exploring Mind	29
• Nature – Mother Nature	31
• A Step of Boldness	33
• Social Inequality Acts 2:44-46-Acts 4:32-35	34
5 - Some of The Discoveries That Prompted My Change	43
Part 2 What Has Changed?	57
6 - Changed Beliefs About the Bible, Jesus and God	59
• The Bible	60
• The Jesus of History	62
• Precious Spirit - God	65
o Spirit of Unconditional Love	67
o Spirit of Light	68

- Spirit of Life   69
- Spirit of Nature   70
- The Fruit of The Spirit   70

7 - Other Beliefs and Thoughts   73

Part 3 An Alternative   79

8 - Is There a True Religion?   81

9 - Getting Together   87

10 - Be Careful Don't be Deceived   91

Conclusion   93

Appendix   95

Some Foundational Beliefs Are Necessary

Prologue

There are many different reasons why people will read this book. Some people are curious about the topic and just want to know what it's all about. An atheist friend who has read some of this book was quite fascinated by it and told me she never knew this is what Christians believed. Others are themselves questioning their beliefs and hope to find some guidance through this book. And then others want to counter what I've written, especially the section on my discoveries and new beliefs. Whatever the reason, I hope this book will give a glimpse into the life of a person who was brave enough to question his Christian beliefs and then change to a new and different spirituality.

The last section does provide a healthy alternative but should be started small. It is only a guide and can be altered according to needs and the type of people gathering.

This book is written in a general and informal way with not many cross-references. It is written as if I am speaking with someone in a park or restaurant. Therefore I trust it will be comfortable to read.

I hope this book will enlighten you and give you an understanding of the availability and the worldwide reach of the Precious Spirit, with no strings attached.

Part 1

History and Influences

1 Where Am I Now?

The change definitively began at a Christian Men's breakfast in Yangon, Myanmar, where I boldly revealed a secret personal belief. I was invited to speak at this breakfast meeting about my 11 years of overseas missionary experiences. Which I did, but then ended with a shocking and profound statement. It had taken many weeks to prepare for this talk while wondering if I should mention anything about my drastic change. I had a hunch that it wouldn't be received very well, and I would undoubtedly be labelled a heretic. But I had this bottlenecked desire to speak out the truth. For over a year, I discovered that much of what I believed did not actually happen or was not true. I had kept these discoveries a secret for fear of the probable ostracization and rejection I would receive. And there I was, about to expose myself to this probability. I remember while I was speaking, in the back of my mind, I kept repeating, "should I or should I not'. These were primarily missionaries I was talking to, and I was about to tell them that a foundational belief of Christianity I once had, I no longer believed to be accurate. Then towards the end of my talk, I paused, quietly looked at all the men and then took that step of boldness and told them that I NO longer believed that Jesus died for our sins and that people around the world who do not accept and follow Jesus Christ will go to eternal hell. There was a deafening silence, and then came the barrage of statements and rebukes counteracting what I had just said. It was an extremely uncomfortable time for me, but thankfully our time was up. After all was said and done, I went home and felt wounded but yet a freer person. It became a pivotal time in my life, exposing myself and beginning a new, freer spiritual journey since I no longer had anything to hide. But I also knew that situations and relationships were going to be different from thereon. This breakfast meeting all happened in 2013, and indeed it has been quite a journey with hurts, joys and challenges along the way.

So, where am I now on my life journey? Am I lost? Not at all. Have I joined a particular spiritual group or religion? No, I haven't. Am I simmering in hurts from the Christian church? Not even close. Am I floating blissfully in la-la land? Mmm, I wonder what that would be like, but no. It's difficult to pin down where I am spiritually at this moment because I am on a journey in my life, as we all are. Never is a day the same.

But, yes, I have left Christianity. It feels somewhat strange after 37 years of being an Evangelical Christian. Back then, I was very committed to its beliefs. Then for 12 years, I was actively engaged in overseas community development and missionary-pastoral work, hoping to convert 'the lost' to Christianity. I convincingly drew people from many cultures, away from their beliefs and into a belief in Christianity. It has quite a persuasive message, although not altogether true. But now the shoe is on the other foot. I'm not against Christianity, as it teaches some good morals and ethics and has a few warm family traditions. I just don't believe most of its theology. I still have a message but a different one which I describe further in this book.

As I look over the horizon of my life and think of all my Christian friends and acquaintances, I see that most are comfortable with what they believe and probably would never leave Christianity. They are convinced their Bible and beliefs are all true, even the story of Jonah, who was swallowed by a large fish and then, three days later, was spat out alive and well onto the beach! A few of my Christian friends, who know of my change, would like to convert me back to Christianity. They would say the same things I used to say using the same scriptures and phrases. Now I can only listen, possibly say a few things but usually politely move on to a different topic or say my goodbye. The relationships have changed, but I understand where they are coming from because I used to have the same beliefs. Sometimes I carefully challenge their beliefs but to no avail. They don't want to hear about it. So now I respect their beliefs, and we do not talk about religion.

So what do I call myself? Possibly, you might call me a Mystic Spiritualist since I believe in a Spiritual Presence or Energy that is present throughout this earth. Over the years, I have lived with Muslims, Buddhists, Hindu's, Free Thinkers and others and have learned many good things from them. I have also befriended many irreligious people from many different walks of life. These connections have given me a greater understanding of humanity, my role in this life and even some intriguing discoveries about the afterlife. There is a freshness, a new spiritual freedom. Now, my new updated vision of life and spirituality brings me greater peace, most of the time. The challenges and injustices still influence me in life.

People have said to me that what I have done is very brave. I don't fully understand why it's brave because I just did it. When I see something wrong then usually I take steps to correct it. Possibly people say I'm brave because they would not want to dig deeper and expose themselves, as I have done. I am finding that many people just struggle or cruise along in life and do not want to upset the apple cart. They are busy with life and do not have the time to look for answers to their doubts or questions. But for me, I desire to dig deeper, to do the research, and I'm still doing it now.

Most religious people worldwide seem to enjoy following religious beliefs and a structure of activities, rituals and traditions. They feel comfortable and secure with this, and they don't want to believe something different to what they already trust. And this is fine. I love watching and sometimes participating in their colourful traditions, as long as we accept and respect each other. I was part of a religious culture too, and it was great to believe in something and participate in the various cultural activities. Actually, most cultural activities and traditions, minus the theology, can be very healthy for our societies. This has been studied and shown to be true. Therefore I am now freer to engage in the traditions of other cultures and languages.

Changing or leaving a religion takes time and can be somewhat difficult. It seemed to be relatively easy for me, though, probably due to the type of person I am. For many religious people, it is often not until they encounter repeated doubts or mental checks that they begin to examine them. These doubts can be pretty unsettling and could build anguish within them because the very thing they trusted and believed to be true has now come into question. The very foundation on which they have been standing has begun to crack and fall apart. The only options they have, are moving from one remaining foundation piece to another or changing completely and finding new solid ground, a different landscape. This change to a new landscape must provide convincing proof that it is indeed solid and much better than what they stood on before. And this assurance, that it is indeed solid, comes when those doubts, questions and mental checks have been convincingly answered and resolved because of discoveries they made that have enlightened them spiritually and created a joy that overcomes any hurts and challenges of change. This all happened to me, and a new landscape was created as I left Christianity and onto a new spirituality. It has been a big step for me, but I treat it as part of my journey in life as I grow, learn new things and practice what I'm learning. There is a spiritual discipline involved as well because from time to time, I do let the ego or selfishness rule, which has resulted in discomfort or hurt. This I can correct and move on.

Some people have said that my discoveries are not altogether true and come from people who are angry at the Christian church. I beg to differ and tell them that my change in beliefs and new spiritual understandings comes from in-depth research based on mostly scholarly critical thinking Progressive Christian, Mystic, Agnostic and Historian PhD scholars. Add to this research my life experiences, starting with my early childhood influences, which I further describe in this book. As a result of all this research and my 69 years of life experiences, I now have a better understanding of people of different backgrounds, cultures, beliefs and morals. The changed life I now live is freer than what it was under Christianity. There are no more following religious rules and beliefs to please a God and feeling bad when I don't. I live life and enjoy it as best as I can while calling into my life the characteristics and values of what I now call a Precious Spirit. I no longer believe in the Christian male god that lives in heaven somewhere. I now believe this Precious Spirit is present amongst all people on this earth, and I hope to demonstrate that presence throughout my lifetime. Every human being of any belief system can draw from this presence. And, thankfully, we have great people like the Jesus of history and others like him who have demonstrated that presence in their lives and given us a model that we can choose to follow. The challenge for me is that if I choose to model what I know to be true of Jesus' life and others like him, my life on earth might also experience some hardships. Maybe this is why early Christianity gradually transformed into the cosy western Christianity of today. The lifestyle of the earliest Christians was too difficult to follow.

I no longer believe in the rapture or that Jesus is coming back soon (the end times) to establish a new heaven and earth. This common belief has prevented many Christians, even some leaders, from strongly supporting efforts to save our planet today. Therefore, my life and time on this earth are more precious, and I do not want to waste it, or at least I'm trying not to waste it on idle things. Amongst other things, I enjoy hiking and gardening. These activities allow me to be more connected with nature and the environment. We need to respect it, work with it, and not destroy and abuse it for selfish gain. Thankfully, with what remains of our natural environment, it's so refreshing to get out there and enjoy and respect it. We receive so much from nature that we need to return what it needs to continue its natural life cycles.

So I conclude this chapter hoping you have a better understanding of where I am at now, spiritually. There is no definitive answer because my life continues to be a journey of discoveries. But maybe, as I mentioned earlier, you could refer to me as a Mystic Spiritualist or just a Spiritualist.

The following chapters will describe my early childhood and onwards, what influences shaped me, the research and discoveries I made, my changed beliefs and ending with an alternative. You can follow the chapter sequence or jump right into whatever chapter would interest you the most. In these chapters, you should begin to see the threads that brought about my change. Possibly you can identify with some of these.

*****

2 A Short Life Story

So, where did it all start? Well, a bit of my upbringing had something to do with it. I was born in Hamilton, Ontario, Canada, in 1951. Hamilton was a booming city close to Toronto and Niagara Falls. It had a few large steel refineries, one in which my father worked. He was a quiet man, and in his spare time, he maintained the vegetable garden, read many archeology books and painted beautiful scenery pictures. My mother, Ursula, left my father when I was two, and as a result, I lived in daycare centres, often huddled in the corners of rooms afraid and lonely. A few years after the divorce, my father married my stepmother, Gabriela, a nurse and very strict at home. We lived in a rough area of town next to a wholesale beer depot and the railway. I used to walk approximately 3 km to school and back and only encountered a few bad experiences along the way, the worst being mauled by a dog.

My parents were part of the Roman Catholic church during those early years, so I had a Catholic understanding of God. Next to my Catholic school was the Catholic church where I served as a mischievous altar boy scuffling with the other altar boys and sneaking sips of sherry wine. I understood that God was male, powerful and always watched me, noting anything wrong I had done. As I accumulated my sins, I would go to confession and confess my sins to the priest, and then as long as I said my 10, 15 or 20 penance prayers, I felt I was in good standing with this God. As for Jesus, he was different. He was hanging on a cross because he did something which I did not fully understand except that he did some good things, and some people didn't like him and then killed him on a cross. I remember watching a movie on a black and white TV in which a troubled boy went up to his house attic and sat beside an old cross with Jesus hanging on it. Eventually, this statue of Jesus came to life like a ghost and lovingly talked with this boy and helped him. It all looked so natural and gave me hope that this could happen for me too, since I was being spanked a lot at home by an angry and strict stepmother, especially when my school grades were low. My half-brother was also experiencing similar spankings but not as frequent. As a result of watching this movie, I would jog to the Catholic church in the evening and light a candle, kneel at the altar and talk to the statue of Jesus, hoping he too would come to life and help me. Well, it never happened. But my school grades did improve a little. As for Mother Mary, I did not understand her position very well except that she gave birth to Jesus and was a very holy woman. I did pray to her from time to time, but I don't think anything special happened.

This Roman Catholic upbringing was my early spiritual foundation, and it certainly taught me right from wrong and that God was watching me.

Some of my fondest childhood memories are those of my Aunt Cilly from my dad's side. She was such a good, kind and loving woman who invigorated me when we went to her home, not just with love but also with plum cake and chocolate marble almond cake. I discovered in later years that she regularly prayed for me. Her children, my cousins, gave me a lot of joy as they were fun and refreshing.

Other fond memories during my pre-teens are the times I spent in the bush looking for and identifying birds and collecting leaf samples of as many trees as I could identify. I even had a leaf and flower press naming everything I collected within the forests around Hamilton, Ontario.

At the age of 12, I ran away from home for fear of what my stepmother would do after receiving a low score of fifty-two per cent on my school report card. I walked all night to a place called Dundas near Hamilton Ontario and waited by the railway tracks near a train station, hoping to hop onto an empty boxcar and ride away to a better place. I had seen someone do this on TV, but no train came and eventually, after many cold hours, I made my way to an apartment block where I cuddled under the stairway and slept for a few hours. Eventually, I made my way back home to some very shocked and worried parents. As a result of this excursion, the spankings became less frequent, and life at home was a little better; however, the abuse from my stepmother gradually returned. In her defence, there were some good times at home too, and I'm sure she did her best to raise us. From what I was told about her life, it was horrible when she was young, being lonely and hurt many times. My dad was a warm quiet man and patiently endured a lot.

During my high school years, I found that sports such as lacrosse, soccer, waterpolo, swimming, and cross-country racing, was a way of staying away from home longer and hanging around with others.

In the middle of grade 11, when I was close to turning 16, I decided to leave home and stay at a friend's place in their basement room. Life at home was still not pleasant due to my stepmother's anger. I eventually found a job with the nickel mines in Sudbury, Ontario. But to get this job, I needed to weigh 150 lbs (68kgs), and I only weighed 148 (67kgs). So, before the job interview, I put lead weights in the inside of my overcoat pockets and then secured the job. It was a difficult job, though, and after unsuccessfully working the 100-pound handheld drill machine at the rockface, they demoted me to directing underground traffic. Despite living and working with many rough men, I managed not to get involved in the fights, drugs and alcohol.

After six months of very tedious work, I quit and hitch-hiked across to Calgary, Alberta, Western Canada, learning more of the hard knocks of life. During these early years, I became an anti-capitalist as I saw the injustices and inequalities in our society and overseas. I had long hair and was kind of a hippy since most of the hippies were the people who wanted a change in the world.

In Calgary, during the winter, I found a very basic room to rent and cooked my hotdogs, beans and buns on top of the oil heater. As my money was running out, I had to occasionally steal some food until I finally found a job with an oil exploration company in Northern Alberta, working as a drill shaft labourer. It was very cold and hard work. Money and food were good, but the after-work environment was a challenge. When the spring thaw came, I moved back to Calgary, Alberta, working as a carpenter and then decided to take some courses at Mount Royal College as a probation student in preparation for university. But due to the lack of direction for my life and other influences, I did not complete the courses. By this time, my parents and half-brother had left Canada and moved to Germany. In a way, this was a little disappointing, but overall it didn't bother me that much since I had become independent. By now, I had taken on some of the roughneck foul language characteristics of those around me. I still had a belief in the Catholic version of God, but my church attendance and confession times were nil.

Then at the age of 21, I decided to get out of this roughneck lifestyle and moved to the mountainous and beautiful town of Banff, Alberta, to enjoy the outdoors. Here I worked as a cook, having learned to cook from my dad. It wasn't long before I met a wonderful woman at the Banff Springs Hotel. Today, she is still my beautiful wife. Her delightful character began to smooth the rough edges in my life. We enjoyed the nature and beauty of the mountains around us and hiked, climbed, canoed and biked as much as we could. In my mind, I was not only close to my girlfriend but also close to Mother Nature (God). The outdoor influences of my early life came back to me. Mother Nature (God) was so present.

After working in Banff, Alberta, we travelled to Long Beach on Vancouver Island, B.C., where I maintained the highway with the Transport Department near Ucluelet. My wonderful partner worked as a waitress at the seaside Wikinnish Lodge. We rented a room in an old house next to the beach. It had a homemade natural woodfired cedar sauna which we steamed up real hot, and then we would run into the cold ocean, an exhilarating experience. After a season on Vancouver Island, we moved to Whistler B.C., where I built ski chalets, and my partner worked at Whistler Mountain Ski resort selling day tickets. During our off-hours, we would ski the beautiful mountain slopes. I can still remember going up the chair lifts and looking out upon the snow-covered forests and mountain peaks and thanking Mother Nature for such beauty. It brought me great joy. The low-level language I had before had disappeared.

After working at the Whistler Mountain Resort for a year, my partner decided to finish her university degree. And so she returned to finish her studies at the University of Toronto, while I travelled throughout Germany, Holland and France. During this time, our relationship had taken a bit of a downturn. But then, upon returning to Canada, I met her at the Toronto airport with a bouquet of tulips. I was hoping our relationship would be restored, and it was. I decided that I too would apply to a university and so was accepted as a mature probationary student at Trent University in Peterborough, Ontario. A few years later, my wife graduated from the University of Toronto, but I only completed two years of university and had to leave due to a lack of finances. This departure was quite disappointing for me, especially after being part of two Geography expeditions, one into the alpine regions of the Selkirk Mountains in B.C. studying alpine plants and the other into central Labrador surveying ice flow damage. However, disappointing as it was, it was a great experience having learned a lot. It was during this time, in 1976, that my partner and I had a pot-luck wedding in Peterborough, Ontario.

While studying at Trent University, a young couple introduced me to Jesus Christ and Christianity. Although I had been raised as a Catholic Christian, I noticed that they had some interesting beliefs, especially one in which they believed the only way to heaven and God was through Jesus Christ. I had been taught it was through the Catholic Church. After many questions about their Protestant Christian beliefs, I eventually became a Christian. My wife became involved in the discussions, and a year later, she too became a Christian. After many church gatherings, I was beginning to put together the bits and pieces of this Christian religion. But I still had many questions.

Having left Peterborough, Ontario and travelling to western Canada in 1979, we bought 20 hectares of land near the small town of Tete Jaune in the Rocky Mountains of British Columbia. We built a log and wood frame house complete with twelve purebred goats, honeybees and an organic garden. I worked as a forester with a lumber company, and our first two daughters were born in nearby towns. This cosy home had become our own beautiful and peaceful Shangri-La. We attended a warm and friendly Apostolic Christian church, and then one Sunday, a visiting missionary convincingly challenged us. He gave a call to go into all the world and preach the gospel of Jesus Christ to the 'lost'. As a result of this 'call', in 1981, I decided to leave my forestry job, rent the hobby farm and attend a Bible College in Caroline Alberta. I graduated from Bible College but sensed I still needed more training to work full-time as a missionary overseas. By this time, our third daughter had been born in Rocky Mountain House, Alberta.

So we moved to Cambridge, Ontario and completed a Discipleship Training School with a group called Youth With A Mission (YWAM). This training included a two-month training trip to Belize and Guatemala to help the poor. After this, we travelled to Tacoma, Washington and completed another YWAM Long Range Development Course, which included training in Haiti and the Dominican Republic. It was here that I contracted Typhoid Fever and felt like I was going to die, but it would be for the Lord if I did. I survived. Finally, I took other International Development and Primary Health Care courses at William Carey University in Pasadena, California.

Once I completed all this training in 1985, our family of three daughters, 3, 6 and 7, left for Pakistan to be full-time missionaries under the guise of Development Workers. We initially worked with the Afghan refugees and then the Hunza Valley people of far north Pakistan. In subsequent years we worked in Thailand, the Philippines, Mongolia, Malaysia, and Vietnam.

I have written a Christian book (Blue Eyes in a Brown Eyed World- 2007) with photos of our 12 years overseas as missionaries.

Our family members were quite surprised and somewhat shocked, hurt and worried at what we were embarking on with our three young girls. At that time, we felt that God wanted us to do this work, and we wanted to surrender our all to Him. This surrendering is what we were taught to do. It showed our commitment to God. However, our family members and relatives did not understand this and were concerned.

For 11 years, I worked as a missionary and pastor, and although developing various community health-related projects, I was also involved in evangelism and preaching. One of my aims, at that time, was to present the message about Jesus dying for our sins so we could be with God when we die or be eternally separated in hell. As we moved from country to country, I shared and taught this message, and many other evangelical Christian messages, to thousands of people in S.E. Asia, Canada and later Australia.

In early 1996 while living in Penang, Malaysia, where our children were attending a private Christian school, our eldest daughter had graduated from high school with honours. After looking at universities in Canada and Australia, she decided to enrol in a university in Perth, Western Australia, as it had a health promotion course. As a result, in late 1996, after a brief stay in Canada, our family emigrated to Australia to help our daughter settle into the western and university life in Perth.

After working a year for a sponsoring church in Perth, I had to find other work. It wasn't easy because my resume mainly had references to overseas community development types of work. So I took a course to teach English to migrants and also bought a TV-Telephone installation business.

After a few years of attending a charismatic church, I was beginning to question the format and structure of the church. It was top-heavy, with most of the attendees listening but not doing. Then I discovered House Churches. I felt that house church was closer to what early Christianity was like in that everyone in the group participated in the meeting, then had a community meal and helped each other when needs arose. These house church gatherings all happened around 2010 when I was beginning to doubt some of my religious beliefs and was searching for answers to those 'secret 'questions. It was not easy for me because I was in a predominately Christian environment, and most of my friends and all my family were Christians. So the answers came slowly. It was a process. Sadly, due to this questioning, we had to leave the group.

Then in 2013, we joined Australian Volunteers Int'l in Myanmar and volunteered under a two-year contract, my wife training teachers at the Yangon University and myself working with two aid organizations. It was here that I stepped onto the springboard toward new religious discoveries and beliefs, thus leaving Christianity.

The following chapter will look at the process of leaving Christianity starting from 2013.

*****

3 My Process Toward Change

As described in the first chapter, the definitive change started after the 2013 Christian Men's breakfast meeting in Yangon, Myanmar. After that meeting, I didn't mention that a young Dutchman approached me and said he agreed with what I said and then began to share some of his doubts and more progressive beliefs. I remember feeling so relieved that I was not alone and finally meeting another person on a similar spiritual journey to mine. He gave me a book to read, which opened the door to many other critical thinking types of books. As a result of this experience, I began to earnestly delve into my research about Christian beliefs and the history of Christianity in general. Over time my research began to reveal some shocking discoveries, which I briefly describe in Part 2.

So many things, I used to believe, did not make sense anymore. Especially the belief that all those Muslims, Hindus, Buddhists, many who were my friends, and so many others were going to hell if they did not accept Jesus Christ as their saviour. This belief is one of the foundational Christian beliefs. Even many of the Bible stories I had believed I could no longer believe as actually having happened. Was Jonah really swallowed by a large fish and spat out three days later – alive!? Were Adam and Eve the first two people on the earth? Did a donkey really speak? Did this loving God command the ancient Israelites to slaughter 50,000 Canaanites and then move onto the land? Was Jesus born from a virgin woman who God impregnated? Did Jesus walk on water and change water into wine? To all of these and many more, I was beginning to say, 'No, I don't think so'. And then add to all this the questions I had regarding all the suffering in this world. Even as I am writing this, it amazes me that I used to believe these stories as factual. But for 35 years, I did believe them as I preached and evangelised in over seven different S.E. Asian countries, hoping to save people from the grips of hell and come into a relationship with God.

For months I spent every spare moment I had to read and listen to as many critical thinking PhD Biblical and post-Christian scholars I could find. Thanks to the internet, this wasn't too difficult. Most of these scholars had already left traditional Christianity after working either as pastors or professors and teachers in churches, Christian Seminaries and universities. It wasn't long before I started getting answers to all those doubts I had. And this all happened while attending the International Church in Yangon. The most revealing discoveries were about the Bible, Jesus Christ and God, which I describe more fully in Parts 2 and 3. Also, in my research, I made many discoveries about ancient history. It was fascinating, illuminating and what I learned, and am still learning, really made sense.

We did attend church in Yangon a few more times since most of our ex-pat friends in Myanmar attended the ex-pat International Church. But when it came to listening to the pastor's sermons, I just could not tolerate them anymore, especially when the preacher was saying things that I no longer believed to be true. So, my wife and I stopped regularly attending the international church, although we occasionally attended to catch up with friends. My wife was initially reluctant since she loves to sing during the praise and worship part of the service. She also didn't have the same interest in exploring beliefs as I had. We eventually made the complete break from church attendance, possibly because she was embarrassed by my falling asleep during the sermons.

The experience of leaving this social group was a bit of a shock to us, and it became rather lonely. No more attending a vibrant church socializing with friends, singing together every Sunday and eating out after church. Our new routine became entertaining ourselves on weekends by listening to music and teachings via the internet and visiting with two other couples who were also questioning their Christian beliefs. It wasn't long, though, before we befriended other foreigners and our local Myanmar friends. The local friends were Buddhist, and they loved showing us many of their Buddhist temples and sharing the Buddhist stories/beliefs behind all the paintings and statues in the temples. It was another learning curve for me, and I put some of their views into my quiver of discoveries. One of them being the concept of emptying oneself of all the worries, ideas, ego, desires and starting afresh.

As time went on in Myanmar, the gap between what I used to believe and my new beliefs widened to the point that I could no longer identify myself as a Christian. It was a bit like being in no-mans-land, although new spiritual seeds of understanding were sprouting around me. I was now beginning to call the Christian God the Precious Spirit and the Christian Jesus the Jesus of history, conceived and born naturally. It wasn't long before word got out that we stopped attending the international church and that I was changing my beliefs. I began to sense a caution toward me amongst some of our Christian friends. However, this is not uncommon. We know of people who had left their religious group, and the elders from that group did everything they could to get them to return. When they didn't, they were ostracized and completely ignored. Having said that, I know people today who secretly don't believe everything the church preaches, but they still attend church. For the most part, it is to be with their longtime friends and experience social life. One of them has told me he hopes to share his new progressive beliefs carefully with his friends hoping they would change. I couldn't do this as it would take a lot of patience on my part to stay in a church, be able to sit through a sermon and listen to something I no longer believed.

As for my wife's spiritual journey, her journey is similar but not the same. And I respect her for that. She doesn't have an interest in researching religious and spiritual beliefs as I do. She has other interests. Mind you, she is open to listening to many of my discoveries, and at times, we will listen to progressive teachers on the internet. Thankfully, even with our few differences, she has been supportive during this time.

I soon discovered a large and growing number of people, mainly in the western world, who have also researched, taken the bold step, and changed their beliefs. I was not alone! Many of them described themselves as being Progressive Christians or

Mystics or Spiritualists and had similar beliefs. It was so encouraging to discover they were experiencing the same joys, challenges and hardships as I was. As I read their stories, I was able to apply many of their solutions to the rejection and separation I was experiencing. And it felt great to be part of a group again.

After our two-year contract in Myanmar, we wanted to continue our overseas work, so we applied again with Australian Volunteers Int'l for another two years and were accepted to work in southern Laos, a Buddhist culture. My wife was a teacher trainer, and I worked in Community Development and Agriculture. It felt good not to be missionaries anymore with a hidden agenda of converting Buddhists and others to Christianity. Instead, we just wanted to help the people we worked with while respecting their religious beliefs and participating in some of their religious practices. It was such a freeing experience. I could love them as they were. I even started to do early morning meditation and found this to be strengthening. It is like being replenished by the 'Precious Spirit'. I would recommend it.

As with any religious group and people in general, there was some questionable negative behaviour and religious fear. We find this throughout the world. Therefore, I would hope that the good qualities within me would rub off on others, and likewise, other people's good qualities would rub off on me. This happened to us as we were supported by the people we worked with and the people in our neighbourhood.

After two wonderful years in Laos, we moved back to Australia. Presently, we have joined various social groups for exercise, gardening, the ukulele and a field archery club within our local and nearby suburbs. We are making new friends, broadening our minds and having new experiences as we mix with a wide variety of people. We also spend a lot of time in nature as we hike and bike the many trails here in Northern Queensland. I continue to practice meditation and learn more about spirituality.

The following chapter will describe some of the catalysts or influences of my life that helped develop me into a person who could change his religious beliefs.

*****

4 Past Influences Guided My Change

I believe that past influences in our lives, generally speaking, will affect aspects or characteristics of our present life even if our environment has changed. And I'm convinced that I've had past influences from my childhood onwards that have motivated me to leave Christianity.

So, what were these influences or experiences of my earlier life?

I can think of four influences that guided my change. The first one being 'The Exploring Mind'.

1. The Exploring Mind

I believe my dad's love of research into ancient history impacted me when I was young. He read so many books about ancient societies and archeology. As I grew older, I too began to read these books discovering how people back then lived, and I marvelled at what they had built. Even today, I continue to watch many documentaries on TV or YouTube about the discoveries archeologists have made, especially those discoveries that reveal how ancient societies lived and how they built those massive structures and temples without our modern technologies. I want to know what made them tick, what they believed. I marvel at their wisdom

Another facet of my exploring mind is my curiosity about rock and boulder formations or strata layers along cliff sides while hiking along a trail or river valley. I will often stop and try to figure out how the ancient forces of nature shaped them. That's why I did so well in geography at university, studying the land formations and how they came to be. I recently hiked to the bottom of a deep canyon and stood on a large 2-3cm brown layer of rock embedded on top of a deep layer of white sandstone. According to the tourist guidebook, this bottom layer was over 2 million years old. Back then this brown layer was the topsoil, and the sun was shining on it. And there I was, standing on it with the sun shining on it again. So amazing.

At times, this exploring mind I have is a bit of a burden for me. I frequently clock up so much time researching prices, products, possible scams, and what information is true or false. I'm an explorer and researcher and naturally dig deeper.

Today I have a service called 'Investigative Research 'where I will research any topic or need for those who just do not have the time to do it themselves.

This desire to do research and explore has been with me all of my life. It has been a catalyst influencing me to question and do research about Christianity.

2. Nature, Mother Nature

My parents and I would regularly visit the Botanical Gardens in Hamilton, Ontario, where I would run along the trails marvelling at the plants, flowers, creeks and waterfalls in my early years. We also spent many summer weekends walking in parks and nearby hiking trails, and during the winter, I would ice skate in the outdoors. It was all so peaceful and brought me much comfort and joy. As the years moved along, I was involved with the Cub Scouts and then Boy Scouts, both of which took me to the outdoors, where I enjoyed all of nature and began to think of it as 'Mother Nature'. I had identified and even leaf pressed many of the regional trees in southern Ontario. Another outdoor passion I had was bird watching, memorizing their names and enjoying all their colours and shapes during the summer and winter seasons. I remember one day killing a colourful bird with a pellet gun and then feeling devastated at what I had done and promising myself never to do such a foolish thing again.

In my early teens, my parents and half-brother often went to our summer cottage at Port Dover on Lake Erie, Ontario. This place provided a sanctuary of peace, and I would wander for hours into the forests with a neighbour's Labrador dog named Sam. I remember sitting in a three-pronged nook at the top of a large pine tree, swaying back and forth in the wind. It was a wonderful experience, and I sensed the presence of Mother Nature.

In my mid-teens, after a summer job, a friend and I embarked on a challenging 5-day hike along the Bruce Trail from Wasaga Beach along the Niagara Escarpment back to Hamilton,

Ontario. The hardest part of the trip was sitting crouched under our very wet sleeping bags while it rained all night. Thankfully a wonderful farming couple invited us to stay with them while they dried our clothes and equipment and fed us more than what we could eat. Although the trip was challenging and somewhat dangerous, it didn't discourage me because I had already adapted to the outdoors and loved being in nature. You might say I was 'one-with-nature'.

As the years progressed into adulthood, I was involved in camping, biking, canoeing and hiking, especially after moving to Western Canada. During this time, I became aware of some of the environmental damage in Canada and other parts of the world, which made me a little angry as the very thing I loved was being damaged or destroyed.

When I became an Evangelical Christian, the environment was still a concern, but gradually my focus changed to getting people saved or converted to Christianity. My love for nature and desire to protect the environment was still there but not as pronounced. I can still remember many times over those years experiencing moments of ecstatic praise while looking at something beautiful within nature.

Then after spending 12 years overseas as missionaries and a short time in Canada, in 2004, we permanently emigrated to Perth, Australia. My focus on the outdoors and the environment returned as we embarked on many hiking and camping trips, and I loved taking photos of the seasonal flowers. Today I have thousands of flower photos. I marvel at their beauty and all their colours and shapes. I sense the Spirit of Nature had something to do with the evolution of all these different flowers

But it was a bit of a challenge going to church. The churches I knew of did not seem as interested in nature or the environment as I was, although a few people did. From what I saw, these churches were more interested in getting people 'saved', receiving the tithe (funds) and nurturing the flock. This lack of interest in the environment disappointed me, and the seeds of discontent started to develop.

Over the years, I learned about and supported some of those involved in sustainable agriculture and permaculture, a system whereby humans, animals, plants, and water work together with nature's processes and ecology. I believed then and still do today that we must treat and respect the environment as if it was our best friend. Some of my friends would say I was becoming New Age or a Greeny, which has negative connotations. But I would assure them I was becoming closer to God. I hope that those in leadership would also love nature and allow it to influence them to make the right decisions concerning our environment.

I believe my love with nature and desire to protect the environment, all of which originated from when I was young, influenced my reaction towards Christian Churches, which did not seem to be as concerned about the environment. I sensed then, when I was young, and still do today, greater closeness to God/Spirit through nature.

3. Boldness

All through my missionary years overseas, I had a zeal and boldness to share the Christian gospel. It was easy for me to do this as I had no fear of approaching people. Even as an evangelist, I would boldly speak on stage at public meetings. This boldness stayed with me even when we left the missionary life and moved to Australia. I spoke at many churches, and even developed seminars and spoke at public events.

As I have already shared, the defining point when I started to change my Evangelical Christian beliefs was in 2013 when I was asked to speak at a Christian Men's breakfast in Yangon, Myanmar. I took that bold step and exposed one of my changed beliefs. This boldness at that men's breakfast and the boldness as a missionary and later seminar speaker was another catalyst that gave me the impetus to move ahead and eventually leave Christianity.

4. Social Inequality, Equity and Acts 2:44-46-Acts 4:32-35

This topic can generate a long discussion that will usually not come to a unanimous agreement. What some think is social inequality, others believe it is not. How this topic of social inequality, social equity and Acts 2:44-46 influenced me to leave the church can be questionable too. But it did guide my decision. As you read the examples I give, you might think I was pedantic or unrealistic when comparing the two different world views. And that's fine. But during my time as a missionary, I did see a difference between what I had learned during my missionary training at William Carey University and what I witnessed overseas and elsewhere. And it did affect my questioning and, later, change.

As I describe this fourth influence, its setting is the years working as a missionary and pastor in Pakistan and S.E. Asia and then the years after immigrating to Australia from Canada.

Let's begin with a definition of social inequality. The following comes from a paper written by Ashly Crossman on January 28, 2020, on the website: www.thoughtco.com. It's titled, 'The Sociology of Social Inequality'. Here is a quote from her article, *"Social inequality is characterized by the existence of unequal opportunities and rewards for different social positions or statuses within a group or society. It contains structured and recurrent patterns of unequal distributions of goods, wealth, opportunities, rewards, and punishments."*

We can see this social inequality both in our western societies and in the developing world. It is at many different levels of society, and I'm sure that most people would rather have a comfortable, healthy and more prosperous life. But they can't. Add to Social Inequality the term, Social Hegemony, which is, briefly, a system whereby the ruling or upper class keep their positions of power, authority and prestige by controlling or influencing those under them. I see this everywhere.

In some cases, the 'well-to-do' were born into it or worked hard with integrity to get to a wealthy position. Others became rich by other means. But what are they doing with their wealth, especially when so many needy and capable people are around them? Is giving the biblical 10% enough? Certainly not. Some wealthy philanthropists give large amounts of money and resources to those who need help, but, sadly there aren't enough philanthropists. Social equality or equity does not seem to be a desire of most wealthy people.

Let's have a look at Acts 2:44-46. This bible scripture is taken from the NIV version of the Bible: *"All the believers were together and had everything in common. They sold property and possessions to give to anyone who had need. Every day they continued to meet together in the temple courts. They broke bread in their homes and ate together with glad and sincere hearts."* I think we should also add the following from the same version of the bible:

Acts 4:32-35 *"All the believers were one in heart and mind. No one claimed that any of their possessions was their own, but they shared everything they had. (* With great power the apostles continued to testify to the resurrection of the Lord Jesus). And God's grace was so powerfully at work in them all that there were no needy persons among them. For from time to time those who owned land or houses sold them, brought the money from the sales and put it at the apostles' feet, and it was distributed to anyone who had need".* * I believe, as do other scholars, the underlined section was added later.

Matthew 19:21 *"Jesus answered, "If you want to be perfect, go, sell your possessions and give to the poor, and you will have treasure in heaven. Then come, follow me."*

These scriptures certainly paint a different picture compared to social inequality. Most scholars agree that at that time, the new believers were overly excited about their spiritual leader, the Jesus of History, because of what he was doing with them and for them including healings. Therefore, they responded as they did with great love and unity in the community. Then as the decades progressed, one doesn't hear very much of this same selfless and giving lifestyle, except for a few individuals and groups. It seems it was too difficult to follow this way of life, and gradually early Christianity began to change. But the essence of these scriptures has been and still is relevant for today. Namely, to share, give, be generous and, if possible, to have a community mindset. Is this what the people of this world, including the wealthy, should do today? Well, yes!

My Social Inequality Experiences

Throughout my teen years and up to being a Christian and missionary, I saw many social inequalities.

Unusual as it was at an early age, I was already thinking about the injustices and inequalities in our world, which gave rise to my desire for justice and equality. As the years progressed, I leaned towards aspects of anti-capitalism as I continued to see many of the injustices stemming from both the wealthy and not so wealthy, greedy and corrupt sectors of our society. This was during my 'hippie 'years.

Into adulthood and after becoming a Christian, I noticed some inconsistencies within the teachings and lifestyle of the churches. In Bible College at Caroline, Alberta, I discovered Acts 2:44-46, which profoundly impacted me. I remember asking a few teachers at Bible college why these scriptures were not being practised. The standard response was that those activities were relevant back then but not for today. This response did not convince me because the giving and sharing of some of our possessions, even some of our wealth, for the common good of all, can be done at any time. This scripture was always in the back of my mind and certainly influenced how my family and I lived.

After Bible College, I knew we would go overseas to be community development missionaries, helping the poor and disadvantaged. So I attended a Christian university in Pasadena, California, that focused on Community Development for the poor. Part of the curriculum included a unit that taught cross-cultural communication and bonding. Cross-cultural communication is adapting to another's cultural level of understanding or worldview to be understood and to understand them better. Bonding is when your lifestyle (clothes, vehicle, food) is close to the people's standards with whom you are living and working. These were key to our work, but more importantly, these were characteristics I saw in how Jesus and his initial followers lived, and I wanted to model it while keeping in mind Acts 2:44-46.

Over those 12 years of working in S.E. Asia, I noticed that many western missionaries working with the poor did not follow the cross-cultural and bonding principles. They lived very well in secure compounds or had large homes with servants, nice cars, and had good healthcare, and their kids were in an International school elsewhere. In a few cases, it was the picture of colonialism. This affluent lifestyle disturbed me. I felt that these missionaries should at least adjust to a similar lifestyle to the locals, showing equality. The Jesus we were supposed to follow did this. A few families we knew had shipped a container complete with a washer, dryer, furniture, cases of peanut butter and jam, etc. They had created an upper-class cocoon that the locals loved to visit. Many of the locals who became Christian did experience an improvement in their lives due to the missionaries inputs. Unfortunately, a large number also became financially dependent on them.

Overall, very few missionaries bonded or used cross-cultural principles. Only a few bonded as much as was possible.

Throughout those years, I did what I felt was right while trying not to be too judgmental. From time to time, the missionaries invited us to their lovely homes, and I had to accept it as it was. And so, for over twelve years, while working overseas in Pakistan, Thailand, the Philippines, Mongolia, Malaysia, and Vietnam, we did what was possible to practice social equality.

Then in 2004, after we permanently moved to Perth, Australia, I began to see some troubling inequalities in the churches we attended. Many of the wealthy remained wealthy, and the poor remained poor. After a church service, most people went home to their everyday lifestyles, some basking in peaceful comfort, others worried about having enough money to buy food or pay the bills and the rest managing OK. It wasn't the same degree of social inequality we saw overseas, but it was similar. We were in the OK group and did help and support a few families who were struggling. Possibly the provision of a government social welfare system reduces the responsibility of the churches to provide for those in need.

I also noticed that most churches didn't openly challenge and oppose the systems of injustice, inequality, lies and deception in our society. This kind of action is complex and might get them into trouble. But if they did, as Jesus did, then corruption and people in authority and power would be constantly challenged and exposed. I'm sure if this happened in the western world, there would be no tax exemption status for all the churches and their leaders. But the world would be a better place. Thankfully, some do challenge and expose these systems.

As for my wife and me, we sign petitions from time to time, post articles exposing some injustices, buy some food for a poor street person, or help a struggling family (usually a single parent) with their needs. And we do not purchase any products from corporations that we know who are harming people and the environment.

Justice, social equality and equity and as much as possible Acts 2:44-46 - Acts 4:32-35 are standards I desire to uphold, but I need to be wise about how to apply this in daily life.

I would hope that we can join with others who uphold these same standards. To do this with greater ease, I believe we need to firstly release ourselves from the dominance of the systems of this world and realise our gifts, talents and potential. And secondly, I encourage you to call on and incorporate into your lives the Fruit of the Spirit: Love, Joy, Peace, Patience, Goodness, Kindness, Generosity, Wisdom, Knowledge, Understanding, Compassion and Power. These qualities I have seen in many good, kind and helpful people from all faiths in our world today. Both Christians and non-Christians. And I'm thankful for that.

These experiences of social inequalities and equity on the mission field and the western churches in Canada and Australia challenged my Christian beliefs. Eventually, I had to choose at a time when I was already beginning to discover things about my Christian beliefs that were not true. I could continue being a secret disbelieving Christian or leave Christianity. The latter I had chosen, which led me to more discoveries I've made over the years. I will briefly describe these in the next chapter.

*****

5 *Some of The Discoveries That Prompted My Change*

These are only some of the discoveries I have made. There are many more, but unfortunately, I don't have room in this book as I want to keep it small. But the list of discoveries keeps growing. You will notice that I haven't always followed the usual format of citing detailed references. Some I have, and the others are what I know, and I'm writing as if I'm speaking with someone over a cup of tea or coffee.

I should add here that this chapter will probably be challenging to understand for many non-Christians. So, if this is you, feel free to skim or skip this chapter and move on to the next. Or continue reading and make some discoveries yourselves. As for Christians who are questioning their beliefs, this chapter could be helpful.

I'm sure many Christians can argue against my discoveries using the Bible, and that is fine. I have listened to so many debates, and it ceases to amaze me how convincing apologists can sound even on matters that don't make common sense. It's like arguing with someone who believes there are elephants on the tree. When questioning their belief, they would say, "You can't see them because they are hiding very well," and then, "Nothing is impossible for God." It's difficult to convince someone they might be wrong when they don't want to believe anything different. And usually, when they are convinced about their beliefs, any challenge to them will result in building walls of resistance to protect those beliefs. Thankfully, I broke through those walls I had.

Now, while walking on this new landscape of my life it's been quite enjoyable making new discoveries almost every fortnight. Am I confident with these discoveries? Since most of them come from critical thinking PhD theologians and scholars, I feel pretty confident. But what is also essential for me is, do these discoveries make sense. Jesus walking on water does not make sense anymore and didn't happen. Walking towards a homeless person with a blanket and food makes sense and can be done anytime. The sea splitting in two to allow the Israelites to pass through does not make sense anymore and didn't happen. Opposing and exposing injustices does make sense and can be done anytime today.

In Bible College and the church in general, I was taught to have faith in matters I cannot see. Hebrews 11:1: *"Now faith is the assurance of things hoped for, the conviction of things not seen."* NIV. I can no longer follow this teaching because I cannot believe in something that I cannot fathom as possible, such as Jesus walking on water. That's why I have repeatedly said, "doesn't make sense". The only exception to this would be the effects of Positive Affirmations and Energy/Quantum Healing.

The following are some of the questions I often asked myself before I left Christianity:

- If the Bible says God is loving and in control, why is there so much suffering in this world, even amongst Christians?

- When Christians pray for God's direction and guidance for their lives and others, why do some Christians have horrible experiences? Did God orchestrate this?

- Why do some Christians thank God for a blessing or provision while others are disadvantaged or suffer?

- If God inhabits the praises of his people, then why were 68 people killed by a bomb in a church while singing praises to God?

- There is so much fossil evidence of dinosaurs and many other prehistoric creatures that lived on this earth millions of years ago. Yet, there is no mention of these creatures in the story of Noah's ark, in which all living creatures came into the ark before the flood?

- Is the earth only 8500 years old, as many Christians believe? There is so much fossil evidence of dinosaurs and many other prehistoric creatures that lived on this earth millions of years ago.

- If the downpour covered all the mountains in the flood story, then it must have been sweet water. How did the saltwater fish manage?

- How did penguins from the Antarctic, Polar Bears from the Arctic, Kangaroos and Koalas from the island of Australia get to the ark in the Middle East?

The following are some of the discoveries I made.

I'll begin by suggesting that you read the following article regarding many inconsistencies and lack of evidence in the Bible:

https://www.sciencemeetsreligion.org/theology/bible-archaeology.php "*Is the Bible supported by modern archaeology?*" *by David H. Bailey, Updated 2 January 2021 (c) 2021*

In the Old Testament book of Genesis (from the NIV version of the Bible), there are some contradictions regarding the flood:

- Genesis chapter 7:12 reads, *'And rain fell on the earth **forty days and forty nights**.'* But then in 7:24, it reads, *'The waters flooded the earth for a **hundred and fifty days**.'* There is a big difference in the number of days for the same event. It wasn't until after the 150 days and nights that the rain stopped.

- In Genesis chapter 6: 19, God tells Noah, *'You are to bring into the ark two of all living creatures, male and female, to keep them alive with you. **Two of every kind** of bird, of every kind of animal and of every kind of creature that moves along the ground will come to you to be kept alive.'*

But then in chapter 7:2, God tells Noah, *'Take with you* ***seven pairs*** *of every kind of clean animal, a male and its mate, and* ***one pair*** *of every kind of unclean animal, a male and its mate, and also* ***seven pairs*** *of every kind of bird, male and female, to keep their various kinds alive throughout the earth.'* So, is it two of every kind or seven pairs?

- In Genesis chapter 7:19, the earth flooded, and the ark rose, *'They rose greatly on the earth, and* ***all the high mountains under the entire heavens were covered.'*** verse.20, *'The waters rose and covered the mountains to a depth of* ***more than fifteen cubits, (6.8meters).***' If this had taken place, it would have included Mt. Everest, and therefore 6.8 meters above Mt Everest. I don't believe this happened at all, but a major flood did happen back then.

One day my grandson asked me about the flood as we were walking along the beach. I responded by asking him, "If the water covered all the mountains on this earth, then where did the water go to after the flood?"

- There have been many flood stories within cultures throughout history. Such as the Ancient Mesopotamia, Chinese, Buddhists, Hindus, Greeks, Aztecs, Ojibwe/Chippewa Tribe, Aborigines, Norse People, and others who all have a similar or slightly different version of a flood story. Many include a story about judgment. The oldest flood story we have today is from the Sumerian Epic of Gilgamesh dated to roughly 2700 BCE. It tells of a great sage who warned the people of a coming flood that the gods would unleash. The sage then built a sizeable circular-shaped boat to carry his family, food and animals. After many days at sea, he released a bird to search for dry land. This ancient story is remarkably similar to Noah's story.

More recently, many geological discoveries in many regions of the world strongly suggest that after the last Ice Age, around 8500 years ago, there were many violent water flows caused by burst ice dams. As a result, large tracks of land were flooded. What is for sure is that a major cataclysmic event happened thousands of years ago that flooded many parts of the world.

- The story of Jonah, who was swallowed by a giant fish or whale and three days being spit out later alive, is indeed a 'Story' but not an actual event.

It is essential to note that the ancient writers of the Old Testament had an understanding of God but one that was for that particular group and at that time in history and for that specific situation or event. It was not for all time. I don't think parents today would let their daughter go to a temple (church) service with a man of Old Testament ancient times, especially if the man just slaughtered a few hundred men, women and children. And the ancient man believed his version of God told him and others to do this.

The following are some discoveries regarding the New Testament. I'll begin with providing some non-biblical evidence that Jesus did indeed exist:

There was a man named Tacitus, a Roman senator and historian, orator and ethnographer, and who lived shortly after the time of Jesus. He wrote the following regarding a major fire and

Christians: *'[N]either human effort nor the emperor's generosity nor the placating of the gods ended the scandalous belief that the fire had been ordered [by Nero]. Therefore, to put down the rumor, Nero substituted as culprits and punished in the most unusual ways those hated for their shameful acts ... whom the crowd called "Chrestians." The founder of this name, Christ [Christus in Latin], had been executed in the reign of Tiberius by the procurator Pontius Pilate ... Suppressed for a time, the deadly superstition erupted again not only in Judea, the origin of this evil, but also in the city [Rome], where all things horrible and shameful from everywhere come together and become popular.' Annals XV.44, as translated in Van Voorst, Jesus Outside, pp. 42–43*

Two other men have written about Jesus and Christianity. Namely, the great Jewish historian Josephus (37 C.E.–c. 100 C.E.), who grew up as an aristocrat in first-century Palestine, and Celsus, a Greek Philosopher who lived in Rome and wrote a book, 'True Doctrine' speaking negatively about the early Christians and Jesus sometime between 175 – 180 AD. *(This book has been lost, but Origen of Alexandria, a third-century theologian, attempted to answer Celsus's charges in his work, 'Against Celsus'.)*

So, Jesus and Christians did exist at that time.

The following are some Biblical contradictions and discoveries about Jesus Christ and other stories or events:

- In Matthew 2:1, it says that Jesus was born at the time of Herod the King, who had died in 4 B.C. But Luke 2:1-4 describes Jesus being born at the time of the census in 6 A.D, which was at the time of Governor Quirinius.

There is a 9-year difference between the two, and if the Bible is inerrant, as many Christians believe, then this is a problem for them.

- According to the Bible, the earliest witnesses of Jesus were Paul and Mark. Both do not say anything about the miraculous birth of Jesus. Paul describes Jesus as having been 'descended from David according to the flesh' (Rom. 1: 3).

- The author of the gospel of Matthew mistakenly translated the story of Jesus' virgin birth. The author was looking into an ancient Greek translation from Hebrew for a reference to Jesus's birth and found Isaiah 7:14. Little did he know that the Greek translation for the word 'almah' was incorrectly translated as 'virgin'. The real meaning of the word 'almah' is 'young woman'. Therefore, the popular Isaiah scripture should read, … *'The **young woman** will conceive and give birth to a son.'* Matt 1:23, not the **virgin** will conceive.

- There were already other miraculous birth stories at the time of Jesus, both in Rome and other parts of the world. For example:

Romulus and Remus, twin founders of Rome, born of the virgin Rhea Silvia;

The Phrygo-Roman god, Attis, was born of a virgin, Nana, on December 25. He was killed and then resurrected;

Augustus Caesar, who was adopted by his father, Julius Caesar, considered himself the descendent of a god – Venus Genetrix;

In ancient Egypt, Ra (the Sun) was born of a virgin mother, Net; Horus was the son of the virgin Isis;

In ancient Greece, Dionysos was the son of either the virgin Semele or the virgin Persephone. Persephone was also the virgin mother of Jason;

Lao-tzu was worshipped as a god and was, like the Buddha, born under a tree and out of the side of his virgin mother.

Confucius was said to be of supernatural origin. He had 72 disciples, and like Jesus, 12 were close to him;

Zoroaster was born of an immaculate conception;

Plato is said to be born of the union of a virgin and the god Apollo.

You can also read the following web page to get an overview of who was either a 'son of god' or was 'born of a virgin' or both: *https://humanjourney.us/sons-of-god-and-virgin-births/*

- The following is a quote, *'The year 70AD saw the Roman Legion obliterating Jerusalem and its Temple and scattering Jewish refugees throughout the Mediterranean. As the teachings of Jesus spread throughout the empire and as his credibility came into direct competition with other religious figures, stories developed about his birth that sounded strangely similar to the births of the pagan deities that dominated the known world. By the 90s, various versions of Jesus's miraculous birth were widespread, and Matthew and Luke incorporated two of these versions into their Gospels.... understanding of the Judeo-Christian texts themselves, Jesus's virgin birth takes its place among the almost countless extraordinary births meant to engender divinity and importance to political and religious figures across time...'* Felten, David, Procter-Murphy, Jeff, Living the Questions: The Wisdom of Progressive Christianity (Kindle Locations 2814-2817). HarperCollins. Kindle Edition.

- The doctrine of the Trinity (God – Jesus – Holy Spirit as one and the same) was not decided upon until 360AD at the Council of Constantinople and the final form formulated in 381AD by Greggory of Nyssa. Jesus or his early followers did not think of him as being the same as God. This belief was decided some 381 years after his death.

And so today, most Christians believe that there are three persons, all of them distinctly God. But there is only one God. So, there aren't three Gods, but there are three persons who are God, and those three are one God. It still sounds confusing.

- Not all the letters in the Bible attributed to Paul were written by Paul. The authentic letters written by Paul are the following seven: 1 Thessalonians, 1 and 2 Corinthians, Galatians, Philemon, Philippians, and Romans. The other six non-Pauline letters that claim, "The letter of Paul to the …", were titled as such to give credibility to an anonymous writer.

It is important to note here that Paul was quite a radical person. In his earlier writings, such as Galatians 3: 28, Paul points out that there is no hierarchy if you are "in Christ". It doesn't matter who you are or what position you hold. Once you join the Christian community, you are all equal in Christ, male and female. In the Roman world of slavery, patriarchy and patronage, this was very radical and unacceptable. In later non-Pauline writings, this radicalism gets toned down.

- Atonement – Christ who died for our sins. This belief would be a good study starting with Anselm's Substitutionary Atonement, but reading from critical thinking progressive Christian PhD scholars. There are eight different versions of this atonement belief that I know. My thought at this time is that the Jesus of history had died because of the sins of some people in his time, not for all of humanities sins of all time.

- Original sin - No passage or verse in scripture speaks definitively about us being born into a sinful nature. Scripture does talk about the range of sin in this world, but not specifically original sin. There is no documented evidence to support that Jesus believed in it, nor the disciples or the early church. It was Augustine, the fourth-century bishop of Hippo, who introduced Original Sin into Christian theology. The alternative to Original Sin is Original Blessing, introduced by spiritual theologian Dr Matthew Fox, a former priest. He had to leave the Catholic Church after he wrote a book titled 'Original Blessing' back in the 1980s. He believes the Precious Spirit was and still is a blessing for all of humanity and our sacred earth. We can tap into this and be part of it anytime.

- In the book of Revelation, which could be a revised version of an earlier apocalyptic book, the destruction of Babylon the Great in Chapter 18 is most likely referring to the destruction of Pompeii by the volcanic eruption of Mount Vesuvius in 79 CE.

- The earliest New Testament manuscript found to date, Papyrus 52, was written sometime in the middle of the second century. The first book of the New Testament, Mark, was written around 45 AD. Matthew and Luke followed years later. These first bible authors living some 45 to 65 years after Jesus' death were writing from oral accounts of what was being circulated at that time. Most of the population could not read or write, and therefore accuracy was not important. Many of these oral accounts had already been changed and sometimes invented as they circulated by word-of-mouth year after year.

- After the death of the Jesus of history, there developed Christian leaders and groups in the region. Over time there were countless controversies and differences in beliefs, especially regarding the scriptures that were being written or had been written. Then in 325CE, Emperor Constantine called on all the church leaders to convene in the Bithynian city of Nicaea. They fought, argued, debated and eventually created the Nicaean Creed, a statement of Christian doctrinal beliefs. Those who opposed were excommunicated or exiled. Yet soon after this council and even up to the present, we still have endless debates about doctrines and scriptures. There are over 12 major denominational divisions in the world today that adhere to a belief in Jesus. Many others, who believe in slightly different doctrines, also adhere to a belief in Jesus. Then there are hundreds of what some call 'cults' that include a belief in Jesus but have created a completely different religion.

I think it best to stop here with my discoveries as they can go on and on. My suggestion is to read or listen to some books from the authors mentioned in chapter 6 and begin to make your discoveries. It should be enlightening, maybe even shocking.

In the following section, I will be talking about the changes that have taken place so far on my spiritual journey.

*****

Part 2

What Has Changed?

6 Changed Beliefs About the Bible, Jesus, and God

I have shared the various influences and some of my discoveries that have contributed to my change. You might be wondering what has changed. Well, lots. But before I write about some of my changes and beliefs, I must say this first. What I believe now is not set in stone. I am still learning and asking questions and am open to hearing what others have to say. Some people have asked me what scholars have influenced me to change my beliefs? Well, here is a list of some of those more progressive critical thinking scholars:

Elaine Pagels, Peter Enns, Marcus Borg, John Dominic Crosson, Diana Butler Bass, John Shelby Spong, David Felten, Karen Armstrong, Bart Erhman, Benjamin Corey, Rachel Held Evans, Brian McLaren, Robin Meyers, Eric and Carol Meyers, Stephen Patterson and others.

Many of these teachers have come from a religious background and, like me, started to question and then change or alter their religious beliefs. So they speak and teach from experience and have done a lot of the research. Please take the time to read some of their books or listen to them on YouTube. You might be quite surprised by what you read or hear. It could be disturbing but also very illuminating.

So what are my new beliefs? Some I have already mentioned earlier in this book. In this chapter, I will focus on three main topics, the Bible, Jesus, and God or the nature of God.

The Bible

Probably the most critical and challenging change has been my beliefs about the Bible, which is the foundation of Christianity. Every sermon preached, every theological debate, all Bible colleges and Seminaries base their teachings on this collection of writings, the Bible. Even I used to devour the Bible and the interpretations I learned from my flavour of Christianity.

My questioning regarding the truth of the Bible started with the Old Testament Bible stories such as the Flood, crossing the Red Sea, the Exodus, Jonah swallowed by a large fish and many other stories. I began to question them as to their truthfulness and accuracy. Did these Biblical events really happen? I had my doubts. Then came the discovery that the earliest copied pieces of New Testament Bible manuscripts that have been found to date were written some 40 to 85 years after Jesus' crucifixion. Therefore, as I mentioned in Chapter 5, the stories about the Jesus of history were first transmitted orally from person to person, which resulted in changes and additions over time.

The first collection of Biblical writings came from an author named Mark, some 40 years after Jesus' death. Then came Matthew and Luke, who wrote years later and copied a lot of their material from Mark and a lost collection called Q. Around 85CE, another writer named John wrote many things about Jesus for his community. But a lot of what he wrote, the earlier writers did not mention in their writings. This then raised the question, 'Where did John get his information?' It is almost 100 years after Jesus. With all these gaps in years, from the time of Jesus to John, the historicity, authenticity and reliability of the New Testament Bible have been questioned by many scholars and myself. Not everything written in the Bible is universally accepted, except for the baptism and crucifixion of the Jesus of history. These events are widely accepted as having happened.

Much is written and said as to whether the Bible as a whole is historically accurate or not. Many events, I have discovered, did not happen. Instead, they are stories and themes which are true in the sense of having some meaning. For example, Snow White and the Seven Dwarfs is a true story that has meaning for young people but did not literally happen. God stopping the sun at the time of Joshua is a story with meaning but, it did not occur. Some events, such as a great flood, did happen, but not as the Bible records it. Other events such as the plagues of Egypt or the star of Bethlehem were perceived as divine events rather than natural phenomena. Many stories in the Bible are metaphors, parables and have symbolic meaning to them. Sadly a large segment of Christianity, primarily conservative and evangelical protestants, believe that the Bible is from God, and therefore, its content is factual. Science and physics are secondary to the bible stories or not accepted, and the meaning or message of these stories is not truly understood.

There certainly is archeological evidence that reveals the names of some important people found in the Bible and confirms the lifestyles and laws for those periods of time. But many of the dates, locations or numbers don't always match with what is written in the Bible. As a result of all this uncertainty and lack of clear evidence, it would be difficult to accept that everything in the Bible is historically correct and true. But I have noticed if someone desperately wants something to line up with their beliefs, they will find a way to make it happen, even using psychological arguments.

Through my research, I now believe that the Bible (The Old and New Testament) is not the inerrant Word of God or God's Word but rather a collection of writings written by ancient peoples thousands of years ago for a specific purpose or situation during THAT time in history. These letters or books included actual events, inspired stories, made-up stories, later inclusions, poems, parables, metaphors and myths. And many of these carry a meaning or message. Lots of careful and scholarly research has been done that shows this to be true, and I'm sorry, but I don't have the references available to prove these points. Sadly, many religious non-critical thinking scholars, preachers/priests and Christians would strongly object to what I've said here. And I have to accept this. It takes time to change one's beliefs, but only if one wants to.

I would suggest that rather than thinking the Bible is God's inerrant word or God's word, think of it as a book written by many men with some good messages and meanings.

The Jesus of History
Other than the New Testament of the Bible, there isn't a lot of historical information available describing the details of how Jesus lived and what he did. Non-Biblical writers during those

first two centuries, who mention Jesus or Christians, include such names as Josephus, Celsus, Origen, Tacitus, Pliny the Younger, Lucian and the Babylonian Talmud. In later years even the Quran mentions the prophet, Jesus. These non-Biblical writings indeed confirm the existence of the Jesus of history, saying both negative and positive things about him or the early Christians.

Over the past few decades, other critical thinking Biblical writers have come to various conclusions about how they each see the Jesus of history. They describe him as an Apocalyptic Prophet, a Cynic Philosopher, Charismatic Healer, Jewish Messiah, Prophet of Social Change, and Rabbi.

Recently, some critical thinking progressive biblical scholars have collectively gleaned from the Bible what they believe is probably the most authentic about the life and sayings of the Jesus of history. We know that the Jesus of history was Jewish, spoke the Semitic language of Aramaic, lived in the small town of Nazareth, which was close to a large city called Sepphoris, which was a trade route and relatively prosperous. Jesus was a unique and intelligent person; otherwise, he would not have had such a large following.

Regarding his conception, I believe the man Jesus was conceived naturally, not from a spiritual impregnation from God. Most Christians would be shocked at reading this because they believe Jesus was God and man. Or God incarnate. To think of him as an ordinary man would put him at our level. But I believe he was at our level but yet, a unique person. He did many incredible things during his life and developed a good reputation, mainly amongst the lower class of society who began to follow him.

From the non-Christian sources, I have gleaned the following:

- That Jesus was regarded as very wise.
- He was an influential and revered teacher.
- He performed miraculous feats.
- He was crucified.
- He taught about love and purity.
- That Jesus' followers believed He was the Christ or Messiah, and Christians eventually worshipped him as God!

And from Biblical sources, at least those that are probably true, I have gleaned the following:

- Jesus lived and walked closely with his understanding of God which he shared with those around him.
- He accepted, loved and had fellowship with the least, the outcast, the disadvantaged, the rich, the poor, the sick and the healthy.
- Even though he got angry with some people, he loved the people, the good, the bad and the ugly (and the smelly).
- He respected all people, mixed with those one should not mix with, treated women as equals and brought healing to many.
- He wisely and non-violently exposed the hypocrisy, darkness and injustices of his day's religious, commercial

and political systems. For this, he had to be silenced, so he was tortured and killed on a Roman cross. Therefore, he did not die FOR our sins but BECAUSE of certain people's sins.

These non-Biblical and Biblical descriptions of Jesus paint a picture of a person quite unlike any other man of his time. And because he was so unique, offering a lifestyle quite different from other religions of that time, people were attracted to him. These alternative teachings and lifestyles were adopted by many people and gave them a sense of security and community, which became exclusive and eventually angered some authorities.

Today I refer to the Jesus of history as the Spirit of Jesus. After he died, his 3-day old dead body did not rise out of the tomb. Instead, I believe he rose spiritually from the dead, as will happen to all of us.

I know there have been other great spiritual leaders over time, and there are many today as well, but the Jesus of history is the one I know the most about, believe existed and that I can model, to a degree, within this western culture. As I try and model this lifestyle today, I am also learning from other spiritual leaders who, I'm discovering, are also encouraging us to love unconditionally.

Precious Spirit - God

God is a name or concept that carries a lot of meaning for thousands of cultures worldwide. Back in the day, when I was a Christian and missionary, my understanding of God was different from what it is now. I used to believe God was a spiritual male, abiding somewhere up there in heaven, who I prayed to, asking for help, protection, funds, health, or whatever I needed and asking God to help others. The more committed I was to God, the more I could possibly hear from him, and the more I felt blessed. Also, the more I praised and worshipped him, the more pleased He was. God would direct my path in life, and I had to obey and make sure I was doing what He wanted me to do. My famous catchphrase used to be, 'I am the back-seat passenger, God is the front seat driver'. Whatever He wants, I will do. Wherever He calls me, I will go.

I now believe this God is a Precious Spirit, not a man up in heaven pulling strings as to what will and what will not happen on the earth from day to day. This Precious Spirit encompasses Love, Light, Life and the Fruit of the Spirit. It does not direct suffering or happiness on this earth but is present in all places and among all peoples. And possibly, even in our cosmos. I have noticed that some Progressive Christian authors also refer to God as Precious Spirit, Ground of Being, the God of the Universe, the Energy, the Light, the Source. I use Precious Spirit and Yahweh (an ancient name from 600 B.C.) interchangeably. But, I believe all these names refer to the same God, and I know it can be present within us and indeed is present around us. This God then is not just dwelling in churches or cathedrals or buildings, or with certain religious groups, but is present with humanity and nature throughout the world.

What God is Not

After the waves receded from the 2004 Pacific tsunami, hundreds of thousands of people of various religious beliefs had died. Many religious leaders struggled with this disaster, asking, "why". Sadly, some American evangelists said that God was punishing those Muslims and Hindus for the evil deeds they had done. Then in 2005, after Hurricane Katrina devastated the city of New Orleans in the USA, a famous evangelist said that God was punishing the city because of unethical activities. This idea that God is punishing people is not accurate at all. These religious concepts are fabricated, and they certainly are not the character of the Precious Spirit. Even within the Old Testament of the Bible, we read about an angry God punishing people. We can find this within other religions as well. But, again, it is not the character of the Precious Spirit.

In the following section, I will briefly describe, but in more detail, the characteristics I have already mentioned, beginning with Love:

Spirit of Love

I have come to understand the Precious Spirit as pure Love, which is present everywhere to bring comfort and assurance. It can empower us to build good relationships even when others are not so kind or likable. It can also empower us to let go of our ego and selfishness and help, guide or comfort others. It puts a smile on our faces and enables us to appreciate and respect life. This Love creates a strong bond with friends and couples that lasts for many years. Not only is this love expressed from within people to other people, but we also express and feel it as we experience the nature around us. We look with awe at a bright blue Ulysses butterfly flutter around us, or we smell the sharp scent of the beautiful white and pink Frangipani flower. All this, I believe, is within the Spirit of Love.

Today many people don't even believe in the Precious Spirit or the Spirit of Love and yet do outstanding good deeds for others and humanity in general, not expecting anything in return. Even though they don't believe it, I sense that they have connected with the Precious Spirit of Love for that time.

Sometimes I have neglected the presence of the Spirit of Love, choosing to think negatively about someone. This isn't always the best way to live.

Spirit of Light

I sense that the Precious Spirit of Light is to bring illumination or revelation on the one hand and to expose and dispel darkness on the other.

I believe this illumination happened to me as I began to understand better the many facets of spirituality that existed in the world today. This illumination can also refer to anything in our daily lives, such as getting that intuition not to do something or to be cautious about a situation or just getting a brilliant idea or solution to something. I find that when I focus on the Spirit of Light during my meditation times, it does clear my mind and enable me to see things more clearly.

As for exposing and dispelling the darkness, which some people call evil, dark spirits, demons, or Satan, there certainly seems to be spiritual darkness present in this world, resulting in much pain and suffering for millions of people and nature and the environment. This sense or presence of evil, I believe, is the absence of the Spirit of Light. It is not in harmony with the Precious Spirit and even, to a degree, nature. We can counter this evil presence with the Spirit of Light within us and around us. On a few occasions in my life, I have awoken from a restless and fearful sleep and called on the Spirit of Light to fill my life, resulting in a peaceful sleep.

Spirit of Life

I understand that the Precious Spirit of Life could possibly bring healing to people, whether physical, emotional, psychological, or spiritual. As for physical healing, I have personally experienced healing on a few occasions. Now, this might sound strange to some but bear with me. Once when I was having severe head pains in the back of my head, I applied what is referred to as Quantum or Energy healing. Together with the Spirit of Life, I visualized the Life of the Spirit swirling through my head and body, bringing things that were not normal to normalcy. After three days of doing this, the pain was gone. So, does this type of physical healing happen all the time? No. Why not? I don't know, and nature takes its course. But I'm thankful that there are medical doctors with procedures and facilities that can help with this. I apply these same principles when it comes to emotional or undesirable situations in my life too.

Spirit of Nature

As I have already described earlier, from my childhood days, I had a sense of there being a God or what I then called 'Mother Nature' within the environment or nature. To a degree, I still feel this today. I sense that this Precious Spirit of Nature is very much part of our interacting natural ecosystem. The more we embrace the Precious Spirit of Nature, the more we respect the environment/nature around us. It is not to say that all of nature is good and safe for us. There are times when nature can harm us, such as when a poisonous snake bites us, an animal injures or kills us, or a tree branch falls on us. So, what I mean by the Spirit of Nature, is the ecosystems of our environment. Without them, we would not be able to feed ourselves or drink clean, clear water or breathe fresh air.

For now, this is how I understand the Spirit of Nature. Meanwhile, the earth grinds, burps and moans, and together with us humans, there are constant changes to the conditions of the environment around us. All the while, the Precious Spirit of Love, Light, Life and Nature is moving along with it.

The Fruit of The Spirit

I want to add another characteristic, which is collectively called the Fruit of the Spirit. These are: Love, Joy, Peace, Patience, Goodness, Kindness, Generosity, Compassion, Mercy, Wisdom, Knowledge, Understanding and Power (to overcome).

To the best of my knowledge today, all of these, and many more, are present within the Precious Spirit. All of humanity can embrace these to a greater or lesser degree. It's our choice. I heard of a Hindu doctor in India who gave up his affluent practice and moved his medical clinic into the slums of the city where he lived to help the poor and needy. Most Evangelical Christians would say this doctor who prays to Hindu gods still needs to be saved to get into heaven. I believe this doctor is making heaven on earth and has a lot of the Precious Spirit in his life already.

I remember reading about the Aleppo Muslim Clowns in Syria who clowned in dangerous areas of the city. They were bringing some joy and happiness to the children who had lost loved ones. The Precious Spirit was with these Muslim clowns amid all the turmoil and destruction. Sadly, a missile had killed the clowns and others.

I start the day two or three times a week by having a quiet time or meditation and top-up within me the Precious Spirit, speaking out all these attributes and characteristics while mindfully visualizing and incorporating them into my life.

*****

7 Other Beliefs and Thoughts

As a result of my discoveries so far, I cannot see myself returning to what I used to believe. Not to say that I have eliminated every Christian belief. Some of them are universal beliefs that most other religions have as well. Such as being good and kind and loving one another. But as for the foundational Christian beliefs, these I have left, which has had some repercussions.

I have had some nasty things said to me, which is part of changing one's religious beliefs. It hurts, but the joy of knowing the truth overcomes these painful experiences. Life must go on. Knowing the truth isn't enough, though. I must also live out the truth, at least as best as I can. And that isn't always easy in today's busy life. But the challenges I face today help me demonstrate the evolving beliefs I now have. Well, at least most of the time.

The following describes my evolving spiritual and general life beliefs, including a few I have already mentioned. Here are some of them:

- I should give or share where it is needed. Not to receive merit, good karma, divine favour or a tax deduction in return, but to give and share unconditionally, expecting nothing in return.

- We are not all sinners because of the story/myth of the sin of Adam and Eve, but instead, we are special people with unique talents, gifts and abilities. And we all have the potential of being good people.

- That after we die, there is a spiritual leaving of the body and going to another place. Regarding this afterlife, and I'm not a hundred per cent sure about this, I have listened to 3 non-Christian doctors who work with people in palliative care. They have recorded thousands of patient experiences of those who had died for a time and returned to life. Most of these patients saw themselves leave their bodies and eventually went to places where most saw friends, relatives, people they didn't know had died. Many experienced a bright light that radiated love beyond words. All three doctors concluded that death isn't something to fear. And there were no blazing fires in a hell mentioned.

- That there is no eternal hell, possibly annihilation for the extremely wicked. And for the other 'bad' people, perhaps being in a dark place and cringing in the pain of realizing all the bad things one did and hurts one has caused. And then gradually coming into a place of Light and Love. This latter experience was reported by a man who went through a near-death experience.

- The Precious Spirit can be present and indwelling (to a greater or lesser degree) with all people of all nationalities, religions, or beliefs and in every situation in their lives.

There is no formula, ritual, or chant to get the Precious Spirit's attention, embrace, or activation. It is the people's choice to abide with or receive the Precious Spirit, and hopefully, they can become better people and bring about a positive change or outcome in the world within or around them.

- The Precious Spirit does not cause suffering, sickness and either human-made or natural disasters. Most of these are natural occurrences on this earth. Human activities cause some too. Whatever the cause of illness, suffering and disasters, the Precious Spirit is present to bring comfort, healing and love to those who want to receive it. And if people aren't aware of this, then those who have this indwelling of the Precious Spirit's love, light and life can share this with them by helping, giving and comforting them.

- We should live in fellowship and harmony with others of any nationality, religion or orientation and, if possible, in a community mindset.

- We should love one another as much as is possible, live a life with integrity and be able to forgive others and receive forgiveness.

- We can choose to overcome and take authority over evil, darkness or negativity with the abiding Precious Spirit of Love, Light, Life and the Fruit of The Spirit.

- That I/we must take care of this earth and support others who want to do this. Let us non-violently, judiciously and wisely oppose and carefully challenge those who don't care about this fragile earth.

- That I should model the life of the Jesus of history and others like him in today's context as best as I can and be willing to experience the opposition and uncomfortableness as I've already described. I focus on the Jesus of history for my life because he is the one that I have grown up with and know and understand the most.

- I should meditate or find quiet times and empty any negativity, worry, stress and receive love, inspiration, guidance, wisdom, the Fruit of the Spirit, and so much more from the Precious Spirit.

- We could possibly bring various degrees of healing upon ourselves and others together with the Precious Spirit of Life. Some call it Quantum or Energy Healing. Sometimes there is complete healing. Other times not.

- That I/we should be able to defend our lives and our partner, family members and the disadvantaged against totalitarianism, oppression, deception, evil/darkness and that which does not bring peace to ourselves, family, community and country. In other words, anything void of the Precious Spirit of Love, Light, Life and the Fruit of the Spirit. By the term defend, I mean we should do everything we can to negotiate or bring about peace and distributive justice. If that fails, then to legally protect ourselves or choose to allow ourselves to be oppressed.

- That I/we become more active in supporting, working or volunteering with the following: Groups and organizations involved with helping the disadvantaged, either locally or abroad. Groups or organizations that help protect our planet. Groups or organizations that expose corruption and injustices.

*****

Part 3 An Alternative
(What! Another one!)

8...Is There a True Religion?

Christianity has the largest membership globally, Islam being the second. Does size then make Christianity the true religion of the world? Well, no. If you were to read up on Christianity's history, you would discover many horrible things have been done over the centuries in the name of Christianity, resulting in tens of thousands of deaths. Sadly, other religions have done similar things. So if size does not constitute THE true religion, then what does? Well, let's explore.

Let's begin by looking at the word 'religion'. Most of us know that religion is a system of beliefs, practices, traditions and a code of ethics. But I want to go deeper and identify the foundation of all worldwide religions. I call it the one universal Spirit. It seems all religions have this spiritual foundation, the unseen power, the supreme being, the energy or even a place. And all the cultures of the world give it their name or concept. Christians call it or him, God. From this spiritual foundation, we have thousands of springboards or threads of beliefs, each one being different or similar to the other. These I call the world's religions which all originate to a greater or a lesser degree, from the same foundation, the one universal Spirit. Therefore we cannot say any one religion is the true religion. But they do all have degrees of closeness to the character, elements, and values of the one universal spirit that I call, Precious Spirit (Chapter 6). So the question is not which is the true religion, but rather which religion embodies the character, elements, and values of the one universal spirit or Precious Spirit.

This universal Spiritual foundation has given humanity, especially most children, the ability to love and be good to one another regardless of religion. And yet, it is the religious beliefs that distinguish religions from one another and distance themselves from the one universal Spirit. All religions that I know of today have various degrees of moral integrity and codes of good conduct. This has a positive impact on their societies and cultures. During my sixteen years of living overseas within Muslim, Buddhist, Hindu, and other cultures, I have personally experienced that most people are good and lovely people. They had helped us and treated us wonderfully while respecting our beliefs. Yet, occasionally they did promote their religious beliefs, believing it was the correct truth. I listened to what they had to say and, more recently, even incorporated some of their beliefs. But since leaving Christianity, I never thought or proclaimed that my beliefs were the only correct truth. Instead, my beliefs are part of many truths with similar and yet distinct beliefs but the same foundational Spirit.

Over the centuries, Christianity has imbedded a subconscious fear of going to eternal hell if you are bad and the hope of going to heaven if you're good. This belief, coupled with the teaching about a loving God, has strongly influenced people to continue doing good and seems to be particularly persuasive in today's poorer developing countries. You will find this idea of going to a bad place for doing wrong and going to a good place for doing good within most other religions of the world as well. And since most people don't want to go to a bad place after they die, there seems to be an international desire to be good, most of the time. The closer one is to the foundational Spirit, the easier that will be.

We All Believe Something

I once read the comments in a blog entry about atonement, a major theological topic, and decided to stop reading about halfway through the 85 comments. I was quite surprised by the comments. What I noticed was that only a small percentage agreed with what the author had to say. The majority either slightly disagreed or strongly disagreed. All, I assume, were from similar Christian backgrounds, some probably more fundamentalist or conservative and others quite liberal or progressive. It made me realize that Christians all have slightly different beliefs and are at various places on their spiritual journeys in life. No one has the only right belief and the only one truth.

Those who claim their religion is the only correct one have caused many hurts and sorrows. For example, I once received an email from an old friend I had worked with when I was a missionary. After a few email exchanges, I described how I had left Christianity and was onto a new path that brought more significant insights and joy. The following email was his response,

'It sounds like you are in a cult. The truth is your last email was pretty frightening. I could hear Satan in every line. I don't know if there would be any repentance left for you or not, but in case there might be, I would advise you to find it. Don't bother to write again. I'll not answer any email coming from you. You need to move.'

I was shocked and hurt at first but then settled down and realized this is how it is. He is on a spiritual journey quite different from mine. Others have told me; I'm going to hell, I'm lost, they're praying for me to come back and so on. These people are also on their spiritual journey and presently believe they have the right and correct truth, and they won't change. Unless they are open to change and, like me, have an exploratory nature.

My wife and I have recently discovered how certain religious beliefs we had, brought pain and hurt to our non-Christian relatives and families. During our Bible college and missionary training, we were taught to give our all, surrender our lives to God and Christ, going wherever he calls us, forsaking everything for God and Christ. And this we did because we believed we were the true religion. As a result, we missed important funerals and left people alone and puzzled about why we left them, hardly communicating with them. Now, after all those years, we have made amends and are healing those hurts.

From my life experiences, both locally and internationally, I have noticed that we all believe something and favour our particular groups, clubs, sports teams, people, etc. In light of this, I believe it is essential that we respect these differences and enjoy life as best as possible, living in harmony with one another. I have learned so much from people of other religions and beliefs and will continue to learn more. I believe we can glean good morals and reasonable spiritual beliefs from different faiths while being aware of and avoiding other religion's harmful elements and beliefs.

What I now believe is another step on my journey, and I feel confident that it is true for me, at this time, to the best of my knowledge. And I'm sure some people will challenge my beliefs and that's fine and to be expected. Thankfully, we all have available to us the same Precious Spirit as our foundation.

*****

9 Getting Together

I would like to offer an alternative, especially for those who have left or want to leave their particular religion or beliefs. It isn't another religion but rather a community of people getting together with similar spiritual beliefs. And I emphasize community in the sense that people will hopefully share, help, learn and encourage one another. This idea of a community might sound too complicated or even scary since it involves meeting new people. But it only needs to begin with you and another person, possibly a friend or relative, and from there, it will grow.

So, for those wanting to come together with others with similar beliefs, I would suggest initially getting together with a few friends who have the same interest and then, when you feel it is the right time, start inviting other friends. I have done this a few times, and we generally met in homes or parks and community centres or even an office. Before starting the group, we had a hub of 2 to 3 people, and together we would discuss how, where and when we would have our gatherings. Then after a few months, we invited our friends, posted on social media and even put up some flyers. The first gathering was small, with 5 to 7 people, but eventually, it grew to over 15 people. When the group grew to 20 people, another gathering was started in a nearby suburb. We have found it best to limit each group to around 15 people for manageability.

It can be pretty exciting when the group grows, but it can also be challenging, especially if you don't know the new people well. You might be asking; Who are they? What are their interests? Why are they interested? How will they be part of the community? So to lessen any misunderstanding, it would be helpful to give new people a copy of the Foundational Beliefs, which I have listed in the Appendix at the end of this book. These create the common foundation of characteristics and values the gathering can adhere to for the common good of all. Even Chapter 7, *Other Beliefs and Thoughts,* should be helpful too.

The gathering can loosely follow a plan similar to the following:

- Meet and greet and acquaint. Get to know one another.

- Settle down and begin a discussion on a topic that the group facilitator will pick. Some topics could be; discussing what generosity means in and through our lives, does meditation help, how we can help with the environment, how we embrace the Precious Spirit.

- Everyone should be encouraged to say something but not dominate the discussion.

- Anyone can play some music, either by instruments or digital, that possibly complements the topic of discussion.

- Be sure to encourage and comfort one another and be positive. Don't ramble on about negative things.

- Open it up for anyone to ask for help with something. Possibly someone needs help with moving house, painting a room, fixing a leak on the bathroom tap, or personal needs. Always make sure people have written permission to do the task.

- End with a shared meal (Potluck) that everyone has contributed towards. Drinking beer or wine is acceptable, but it is up to the group to decide what alcohol is allowed. Be aware that sometimes people just come for the food and don't contribute anything. It is up to the gathering to decide what to do in the long term.

You want to help build a community of people who will respect one another while understanding different personalities will come together. Love, respect and trust are crucial, and a willingness to give up some of our rights.

Having a vision and plan is essential, and all new people should know what they are joining and what to expect of them in the way of helping, contributing, sharing, etc. Eventually, each gathering would need to discuss how they want to operate in the long term. It is essential to make the gathering a good and healthy fellowship, where people can feel at home and be accepted.

*****

10 Be Careful Don't Be Deceived

Sadly, today's world is full of so many deceptions, scams and fake news that it's getting more challenging to know the truth. The internet has undoubtedly helped propagate these deceptions. Many billions of dollars are taken by evil people worldwide who don't have an ounce of care or concern for the people naively giving them money.

Back when I was a Christian, it wasn't as widespread as it is today. Still, I did experience it personally once within the Christian community when a man had deceived me, claiming a close connection with angels. Eventually, I discovered what was happening and dropped it. I found he had paid $25,000 for a course teaching him how to develop a unique Christian money-making ministry different from others and gradually building a large-paying membership of supporters who also bought his books. Does this sound familiar? It's still happening today. Whether Christian or non-Christian, many forms of spirituality are being used today to make a lot of money. A few of these people even own or lease a jet plane. And hundreds of thousands of people give financially and follow them. These deceptive people prey on people's deep needs. Some even think they are doing God's will.

Then there are the Christian and non-Christian charities and aid organizations. Not all, but some do an excellent job of helping the needs of the poor, sick, hungry, homeless and disadvantaged people worldwide while paying their management mid-level salaries. But, other organizations pay large salaries with all benefits (housing, medical, schooling and vacations) to their management teams. For these charities and aid organizations to prosper and live so well, they need hundreds of thousands of poor, sick, hungry, homeless and disadvantaged people to help.

I once had a client in my Coaching business who wanted me to help her set up an aid organization in S.E. Asia. After a few sessions, I discovered her main objective was to receive a minimum salary of $95,000 per year. I discontinued the sessions. I would often wonder, if aid organization salaries were only between $45K - $65K per year, instead of between $95K to $250K per year, would they still want to work for the cause. I only know of a few who would, but they also evangelise.

When I give to a charity or an aid organization, I will usually ask them for their most recent financial report, which states the staff's salary, and what the directors and management receive. If they don't want to disclose the latter two, then I will not support them.

We have to be vigilant and careful when it comes to spiritual matters. Do your research before giving any money.

*****

Conclusion

Back in 2013, I made a choice that has resulted in an incredible journey of discovery, challenges, hurts and many joys. I chose to expose my new spiritual non-Christian beliefs. It was made with caution, boldness, intuition and enough scholarly research that eventually led me to leave Christianity. I didn't want to live my non-Christina life while pretending to be a Christian. Now, many years later, I still find myself connected to the spiritual realm but with a much clearer and better understanding of what it is. I feel my life has been liberated, and I am generally happier, even though naturally, my life will still have ups and downs.

Recently, a lady asked me if my life has been fulfilling and if I regret having taught what I now don't believe to be true anymore. After some deep thought, I finally answered by saying that indeed my life has been fulfilling, even all those years teaching, preaching and evangelising. At that time, it was fulfilling, and I was happy doing what I was doing then. I helped bring happiness, health and a better life to many people. But, regrettably, many of my Christian religious messages were incorrect. And now, I still feel fulfilled but on a different spiritual platform with new insights coming my way from time to time. It continues to be an interesting journey.

I also want to say that even though I have left Christianity, I do not dislike Christians but respect them and their beliefs, as I do people of other faiths. However, I have issues with extreme fundamentalists.

I hope you have enjoyed this story of my journey and that it has encouraged you and given you a greater love and respect for others, yourself, the environment and the Precious Spirit. Possibly this book has given you that push needed to explore further and get answers to those questions or doubts you may have regarding your present beliefs. To this, I say, 'Go and explore', and probably be shocked at what you will discover, as I was. But there is a richness out there that will enlighten you.

I hope we can live our lives in a way that demonstrates the presence of the Spirit of Love, Light, Life and the Fruit of the Spirit. The man Jesus and others like him have done this, producing positive results for humankind, nature and the environment. Our lives should continue to be a journey as we read, listen, observe and discover new things. And while doing this, to continue loving, respecting, and wisely giving to and helping others as best as is possible.

Cheers and Blessings

*****

Appendix

Some Foundational Beliefs for a Gathering

It seems most people like to be part of something with similar beliefs and a way of life. These similar beliefs are what I call foundational beliefs, and they provide a sense of safety and community when gathering together or helping one another. I have been part of many such groups in the past and found that when new people came and didn't like or agree with our beliefs or way of doing things, we didn't see them again. Foundational beliefs pull the group together on common ground, thus preventing conflicts or arguing.

I have put together a list of qualities and characteristics that should be common amongst the gathering members. Most importantly, we live by example and operate within the presence of the Precious Spirit.

The following Foundational Beliefs have some duplications from chapter 7. You can add others from Chapter 7 if you want.

- We understand that we are on a spiritual journey and know that a Spirit is present throughout the earth and the cosmos. This Spirit we call the Precious Spirit and understand that other people may call it, The Ground of Being, The Source, The Energy, etc.

- We understand that this Precious Spirit has the characteristics or values of Love, Joy, Peace, Patience, Goodness, Kindness, Generosity, Compassion, Mercy, Wisdom, Knowledge, Understanding and Power. These are available to anyone at any time with no special requirements or rituals to receive them.

- We understand the lifestyle of the Jesus of History, as described in chapter 6, is a model we can follow in today's context, knowing it can cause us some discomfort too.

- We believe we should live by example and pass on these characteristics and values of the Precious Spirit through our lives to others.

- We are open to receive teaching and insights from others with similar beliefs, including those outside our gathering.

- We can teach, by example, to love, respect, support and help one another, including others outside our gathering.

- We will practice equality, equity, fairness, justice, forgiveness and humility amongst ourselves and others outside our circle, including those from other countries.

- We should love one another as much as is possible, live a life with integrity and be able to forgive others and receive forgiveness.

- We will protect our nature and the environment and support and help groups actively engaged in doing this. And if it is our field of expertise, we will create or maintain sustainable agricultural and other sustainable living or economic processes.

- We will wisely, effectively, timely, and nonviolently speak out against the injustices, deceptions and corruptions in and around us.

- We will share and give wisely to those in need, even those outside our circle of friends or gatherings. Not to receive merit, good karma, Godly favour or a tax deduction, but to share or give unconditionally expecting nothing in return.

- We will NOT be: self-seeking or selfish, greedy for more wealth, liars and deceivers, two-faced, power-hungry, walking over others or using others for selfish personal gain or wealth, disrespectful of other people both men and women, hurting others physically or emotionally, stealing possessions from others especially the defenceless, willfully destroying or harming our environment, enslaving others for personal gain and or wealth. And the list goes on.

- We understand that meditation or quiet time is exceptionally beneficial for the mind and body. Therefore, we will have periods of quiet time or meditation, at whatever times it feels right for us. Meditation can be done at home or out in the park or forest and for whatever length of time we want. Some people meditate for 15 minutes 3 times a week, others meditate for 30 minutes twice a week, yet others do it every day.

*****

www.ingramcontent.com/pod-product-compliance
Lightning Source LLC
Chambersburg PA
CBHW072059290426
44110CB00014B/1745